# Poems of Friendship

# Poems of Friendship

Edited by Gail Harvey

GRAMERCY BOOKS
New York

Manufactured in Singapore

Designed by Melissa Ring

Library of Congress Cataloging-in-Publication Data
Poems of friendship.
     p.     cm.
   ISBN 0-517-03153-1
   1. Friendship—Poetry.   2. English poetry.
3. American Poetry.
PR1195.F73P64   1990
821.008′0353—dc20                          90-31411
                                           CIP

8  7  6  5  4

# Contents

# Introduction

"*A* friend," wrote John Lyly in the seventeenth century, "is in prosperity a pleasure, a solace in adversity, in grief a comfort, in joy a merry companion, at all times another I." It is no different today than it was three hundred years ago. A good friend, a true friend, is always another you.

A friend can be of the same sex or the opposite sex. There may be a span of many years between friends. Sisters can be friends and so can brothers. And nothing is so precious as friends of the heart—lovers who are also friends. Friendships can be maintained for many decades and despite long separations. A dormant friendship can be reawakened by a letter or even by a chance meeting.

Friendship has always inspired poets. *Poems of Friendship* is a new collection of poems that evoke the joys and the sadness of these rich relationships. Many of the world's great poets are represented here. Aubrey De Vere describes early friendship, "That friendship which first came, and which shall last endure." Julia Ward Howe extols the friend who is "most like a royal guest" and Thomas Moore tells of a joyous meeting with friends of his youth. Joseph Parry applauds friendships that have stood the test of time and John Godfrey Saxe tells with good-natured humor about the friend who never knows when it is time to leave. William Wordsworth writes movingly to a distant friend and John Greenleaf Whittier bestows a loving legacy on a beloved companion.

Included, too, is Henry Wadsworth Longfellow's lovely poem *The Arrow and the Song,* Charles Lamb's lament for *The Old Familiar Faces,* as well as memorable poems by Alfred Tennyson, William Shakespeare, Robert Burns, and Walt Whitman. Also represented are a number of poets whose names have been lost, or were never known, but the sensitivity and insight of their poems cannot fail to stir us now.

*Poems of Friendship* celebrates the wonder, warmth, and rewards of having a friend and of being a friend.

GAIL HARVEY

NEW YORK
1990

# THE ARROW AND THE SONG

*I* shot an arrow into the air,
It fell to earth, I knew not where;
For so swiftly it flew, the sight
Could not follow it in its flight.

I breathed a song into the air,
It fell to earth, I knew not where;
For, who has sight so keen and strong
That it can follow the flight of song?

Long, long afterward, in an oak
I found the arrow, still unbroke;
And the song, from beginning to end,
I found again in the heart of a friend.

HENRY WADSWORTH LONGFELLOW

## A SISTER

*F*or there is no friend like a sister
In calm or stormy weather;
To cheer one on the tedious way,
To fetch one if one goes astray,
To lift one if one totters down,
To strengthen whilst one stands.

CHRISTINA ROSSETTI

## FRIENDSHIP

*O*h, the comfort—the inexpressible comfort
    of feeling safe with a person,
Having neither to weigh thoughts,
Nor measure words—but pouring them
All right out—just as they are—
Chaff and grain together—
Certain that a faithful hand will
Take and sift them—
Keep what is worth keeping—
And with the breath of kindness
Blow the rest away.

Dinah Maria Mulock Craik

# THE ONLY WAY TO HAVE A FRIEND

*T*he only way to have a friend
   Is to be one yourself;
The only way to keep a friend
   Is to give from that wealth.

For friendship must be doublefold,
   Each one must give his share
Of feelings true if he would reap
   The blessings that are there.

If you would say, "He is my friend,"
   Then nothing else will do
But you must say, "I am his friend,"
   And prove that fact be true.

AUTHOR UNKNOWN

# FRIENDSHIP

*F*riendship needs no studied phrases,
   Polished face, or winning wiles;
Friendship deals no lavish praises,
   Friendship dons no surface smiles.

Friendship follows Nature's diction,
   Shuns the blandishments of Art,
Boldly severs truth from fiction,
   Speaks the language of the heart.

Friendship favors no condition,
   Scorns a narrow-minded creed,
Lovingly fulfills its mission,
   Be it word or be it deed.

Friendship cheers the faint and weary,
   Makes the timid spirit brave,
Warns the erring, lights the dreary,
   Smooths the passage to the grave.

Friendship—pure, unselfish friendship,
   All through life's allotted span,
Nurtures, strengthens, widens, lengthens,
   Man's relationship with man.

AUTHOR UNKNOWN

## FRIENDS AND ENEMIES

*H*e who has a thousand friends
Has not a friend to spare,
While he who has one enemy
Shall meet him everywhere.

RALPH WALDO EMERSON

Summer may change for winter,
Flowers may fade and die,
But I shall ever love thee
While I can heave a sigh!

## LOVE OF FRIENDS

$M$ an strives for glory, honor, fame,
That all the world may know his name,
Amasses wealth by brain and hand;
Becomes a power in the land.
But when he nears the end of life
And looks back o'er the years of strife,
He finds that happiness depends
On none of these, but love of friends.

AUTHOR UNKNOWN

## TO A FRIEND

*G*o, then, and join the murmuring city's throng!
  Me thou dost leave to solitude and tears;
  To busy fantasies, and boding fears,
Lest ill betide thee; but 't will not be long
Ere the hard season shall be past; till then
  Live happy; sometimes the forsaken shade
  Remembering, and these trees now left to fade;
Nor, mid the busy scenes and hum of men,
Wilt thou my cares forget: in heaviness
  To me the hours shall roll, weary and slow,
  Till mournful autumn past, and all the snow
Of winter pale, the glad hour I shall bless
That shall restore thee from the crowd again,
To the green hamlet on the peaceful plain.

WILLIAM LISLE BOWLES

## EARLY FRIENDSHIP

*T*he half-seen memories of childish days,
When pains and pleasures lightly came and went;
The sympathies of boyhood rashly spent
In fearful wand'rings through forbidden ways;
The vague, but manly wish to tread the maze
Of life to noble ends,—whereon intent,
Asking to know for what man here is sent,
The bravest heart must often pause, and gaze,—
The firm resolve to seek the chosen end
Of manhood's judgment, cautious and mature,—
Each of these viewless bonds binds friend to friend
With strength no selfish purpose can secure:
My happy lot is this, that all attend
That friendship which first came, and which shall
    last endure.

AUBREY DE VERE

Accept this rose from a fond heart faithful and true.

## THE STIMULUS OF FRIENDSHIP

*B*ecause of your firm faith, I kept the track
Whose sharp set stones my strength had almost spent—
I could not meet your eyes, if I turned back,
      So on I went.

Because of your strong love, I held my path
When battered, worn and bleeding in the fight—
How could I meet your true eyes, blazing wrath?
      So I kept right.

AUTHOR UNKNOWN

# THE ROYAL GUEST

*T*hey tell me I am shrewd with other men;
   With thee I'm slow, and difficult of speech.
With others I may guide the car of talk:
   Thou wing'st it oft to realms beyond my reach.

If other guests should come, I'd deck my hair,
   And choose my newest garment from the shelf;
When thou art bidden, I would clothe my heart
   With holiest purpose, as for God himself.

For them I while the hours with tale or song,
   Or web of fancy, fringed with careless rhyme;
But how to find a fitting lay for thee,
   Who hast the harmonies of every time!

O friend beloved! I sit apart and dumb,—
   Sometimes in sorrow, oft in joy divine;
My lip will falter, but my prisoned heart
   Springs forth to measure its faint pulse with thine.

Thou art to me most like a royal guest,
   Whose travels bring him to some lowly roof,
Where simple rustics spread their festal fare
   And, blushing, own it is not good enough.

Bethink thee, then, whene'er thou com'st to me,
   From high emprise and noble toil to rest,
My thoughts are weak and trivial, matched with thine;
   But the poor mansion offers thee its best.

JULIA WARD HOWE

# AND DOTH NOT A MEETING LIKE THIS

*A*nd doth not a meeting like this make amends
For all the long years I've been wand'ring away—
To see thus around me my youth's early friends,
As smiling and kind as in that happy day?
Though haply o'er some of your brows, as o'er mine,
The snowfall of Time may be stealing—what then?
Like Alps in the sunset, thus lighted by wine,
We'll wear the gay tinge of Youth's roses again.

What softened remembrances come o'er the heart,
In gazing on those we've been lost to so long!
The sorrows, the joys, of which once they were part,
Still round them, like visions of yesterday, throng;
As letters some hand hath invisibly traced,
When held to the flame will steal out on the sight.
So many a feeling, that long seemed effaced,
The warmth of a moment like this brings to light.

And thus, as in memory's bark we shall glide,
To visit the scenes of our boyhood anew,
Though oft we may see, looking down on the tide,
The wreck of full many a hope shining through;
Yet still, as in fancy we point to the flowers
That once made a garden of all the gay shore,
Deceived for a moment, we'll think them still ours,
And breathe the fresh air of Life's morning once more.

So brief our existence, a glimpse, at the most,
Is all we can have of the few we hold dear;
And oft even joy is unheeded and lost
For want of some heart that could echo it, near.
Ah, well may we hope, when this short life is gone,
To meet in some world of more permanent bliss;
For a smile, or a grasp of the hand, hast'ning on,
Is all we enjoy of each other in this.

But, come, the more rare such delights to the heart,
The more we should welcome, and bless them the more;
They're ours, when we meet—they are lost when we
    part—
Like birds that bring Summer, and fly when 'tis o'er.
Thus circling the cup, hand in hand, ere we drink,
Let Sympathy pledge us, through pleasure, through
    pain,
That, fast as a feeling but touches one link,
Her magic shall send it direct through the chain.

THOMAS MOORE

# TO A FRIEND

*Y*ou entered my life in a casual way,
   And saw at a glance what I needed;
There were others who passed me or met me each day,
   But never a one of them heeded.
Perhaps you were thinking of other folks more,
   Or chance simply seemed to decree it;
I know there were many such chances before,
   But the others—well, they didn't see it.

You said just the thing that I wished you would say,
   And you made me believe that you meant it;
I held up my head in the old gallant way,
   And resolved you should never repent it.
There are times when encouragement means such a lot,
   And a word is enough to convey it;
There were others who could have, as easy as not—
   But, just the same, they didn't say it.

There may have been someone who could have done more
   To help me along, though I doubt it;
What I needed was cheering, and always before
   They had let me plod onward without it.
You helped to refashion the dream of my heart,
   And made me turn eagerly to it;
There were others who might have (I question that part)—
   But, after all, they didn't do it!

GRACE STRICKER DAWSON

## NEW FRIENDS AND OLD FRIENDS

*M*ake new friends, but keep the old;
Those are silver, these are gold.
New-made friendships, like new wine,
Age will mellow and refine.
Friendships that have stood the test—
Time and change—are surely best;
Brow may wrinkle, hair grow gray;
Friendship never knows decay.
For 'mid old friends, tried and true,
Once more we our youth renew.
But old friends, alas! may die;
New friends must their place supply.
Cherish friendship in your breast—
New is good, but old is best;
Make new friends, but keep the old;
Those are silver, these are gold.

JOSEPH PARRY

# THE MEETING OF THE SHIPS

*"We take each other by the hand, and we exchange a few words and looks of kindness, and we rejoice together for a few short moments; and then days, months, years intervene, and we see and know nothing of each other."*
—WASHINGTON IRVING

*T*wo barks met on the deep mid-sea,
 When calms had stilled the tide;
A few bright days of summer glee
 There found them side by side.

And voices of the fair and brave
 Rose mingling thence in mirth;
And sweetly floated o'er the wave
 The melodies of earth.

Moonlight on that lone Indian main
 Cloudless and lovely slept;
While dancing step and festive strain
 Each deck in triumph swept.

And hands were linked, and answering eyes
 With kindly meaning shone;
O, brief and passing sympathies,
 Like leaves together blown!

A little while such joy was cast
 Over the deep's repose,
Till the loud singing winds at last
 Like trumpet music rose.

And proudly, freely on their way
    The parting vessels bore;
In calm or storm, by rock or bay,
    To meet—O, nevermore!

Never to blend in victory's cheer,
    To aid in hours of woe;
And thus bright spirits mingle here,
    Such ties are formed below.

FELICIA HEMANS

## CONFIDE IN A FRIEND

*W*hen you're tired and worn at the close of day
And things just don't seem to be going your way,
When even your patience has come to an end,
Try taking time out and confide in a friend.

Perhaps she too may have walked the same road
With a much troubled heart and burdensome load,
To find peace and comfort somewhere near the end,
When she stopped long enough to confide in a friend.

For then are most welcome a few words of cheer,
For someone who willingly lends you an ear.
No troubles exist that time cannot mend,
But to get quick relief, just confide in a friend.

AUTHOR UNKNOWN

*A*gain I hear that creaking step!—
    He's rapping at the door!—
Too well I know the boding sound
    That ushers in a bore.
I do not tremble when I meet
    The stoutest of my foes,
But Heaven defend me from the friend
    Who comes—but never goes!

He drops into my easy-chair,
    And asks about the news;
He peers into my manuscript,
    And gives his candid views;
He tells me where he likes the line,
    And where he's forced to grieve;
He takes the strangest liberties,—
    But never takes his leave!

He reads my daily paper through
    Before I've seen a word;
He scans the lyric (that I wrote)
    And thinks it quite absurd;
He calmly smokes my last cigar,
    And coolly asks for more;
He opens everything he sees—
    Except the entry door!

He talks about his fragile health,
    And tells me of the pains
He suffers from a score of ills
    Of which he ne'er complains;
And how he struggled once with death
    To keep the fiend at bay;
On themes like those away he goes,—
    But never goes away!

He tells me of the carping words
    Some shallow critic wrote;
And every precious paragraph
    Familiarly can quote;
He thinks the writer did me wrong;
    He'd like to run him through!
He says a thousand pleasant things,—
    But never says, "Adieu!"

Whene'er he comes,—that dreadful man,—
    Disguise it as I may,
I know that, like an Autumn rain,
    He'll last throughout the day.
In vain I speak of urgent tasks;
    In vain I scowl and pout;
A frown is no extinguisher,—
    It does not put him out!

I mean to take the knocker off,
    Put crape upon the door,
Or hint to John that I am gone
    To stay a month or more.
I do not tremble when I meet
    The stoutest of my foes,
But Heaven defend me from the friend
    Who never, never goes!

John Godfrey Saxe

## A FRIEND

*T*is a little thing
To give a cup of water; yet its draught
Of cool refreshment, drained by fevered lips,
May give a shock of pleasure to the frame
More exquisite than when nectarean juice
Renews the life of joy in happier hours.
It is a little thing to speak a phrase
Of common comfort which by daily use
Has almost lost its sense, yet on the ear
Of him who thought to die unmourned 'twill fall
Like choicest music, fill the glazing eye
With gentle tears, relax the knotted hand
To know the bonds of fellowship again;
And shed on some unhappy soul
A sense, to him who else were lonely,
That a friend is near and feels.

Sir Thomas N. Talfourd

# I DREAM'D IN A DREAM

*I* dream'd in a dream I saw a city invincible to the attacks
   of the whole of the rest of the earth,
I dream'd that was the new city of Friends,
Nothing was greater there than the quality of robust love,
   it led the rest,
It was seen every hour in the actions of the men of that city,
And in all their looks and words.

WALT WHITMAN

# IF YOU BUT KNEW

*I*f you but knew
How all my days seemed filled with dreams of you,
How sometimes in the silent night
Your eyes thrill through me with their tender light,
How oft I hear your voice when others speak,
How you 'mid other forms I seek—
Oh, love more real than though such dreams were true
If you but knew.

Could you but guess
How you alone make all my happiness,
How I am more than willing for your sake
To stand alone, give all and nothing take,
Nor chafe to think you bound while I am free,
Quite free, till death, to love you silently,
Could you but guess.

Could you but learn
How when you doubt my truth I sadly yearn
To tell you all, to stand for one brief space
Unfettered, soul to soul, as face to face,
To crown you king, my king, till life shall end,
My lover and likewise my truest friend,
Would you love me, dearest, as fondly in return,
Could you but learn?

Author Unknown

# ANY WIFE OR HUSBAND

*L*et us be guests in one another's house
With deferential "No" and courteous "Yes";
Let us take care to hide our foolish moods
Behind a certain show of cheerfulness.

Let us avoid all sullen silences;
We should find fresh and sprightly things to say;
I must be fearful lest you find me dull,
And you must dread to bore me any way.

Let us knock gently at each other's heart,
Glad of a chance to look within—and yet
Let us remember that to force one's way
Is the unpardoned breach of etiquette.

So shall I be hostess—you, the host—
Until all need for entertainment ends;
We shall be lovers when the last door shuts,
But what is better still—we shall be friends.

CAROL HAYNES

## A WARM AND FAITHFUL FRIEND

*I* want a warm and faithful friend,
    To cheer the adverse hour;
Who ne'er to flatter will descend,
    Not bend the knee to power.
A friend to chide me when I'm wrong,
    My inmost soul to see;
And that my friendship prove as strong
    To him as his to me.

JOHN QUINCY ADAMS

# THE QUARREL OF FRIENDS

*A* las! they had been friends in youth:
But whispering tongues can poison truth;
And constancy lives in realms above;
   And life is thorny; and youth is vain;
And to be wroth with one we love
   Doth work like madness in the brain.
And thus it chanced, as I divine,
With Roland and Sir Leoline!
Each spoke words of high disdain
   And insult to his heart's best brother;
They parted,—ne'er to meet again!
   But never either found another
To free the hollow heart from paining.
They stood aloof, the scars remaining,
Like cliffs which had been rent asunder;
   A dreary sea now flows between,
But neither heat, nor frost, nor thunder
   Shall wholly do away, I ween,
   The marks of that which once hath been.

SAMUEL COLERIDGE

# FRIENDSHIP

*D*ear friend, I pray thee, if thou wouldst be proving
 Thy strong regard for me,
Make me no vows. Lip service is not loving;
 Let thy faith speak for thee.

Swear not to me that nothing can divide us—
 So little such oaths mean.
But when distrust and envy creep beside us,
 Let them not come between.

Say not to me the depths of thy devotion
 Are deeper than the sea;
But watch, lest doubt or some unkind emotion
 Embitter them for thee.

Vow not to love me ever and forever,
 Words are such idle things;
But when we differ in opinions, never
 Hurt me by little stings.

I'm sick of words: they are so lightly spoken,
 And spoken, are but air.
I'd rather feel thy trust in me unbroken
 Than list thy words so fair.

If all the little proofs of trust are heeded,
 If thou art always kind,
No sacrifice, no promise will be needed
 To satisfy my mind.

ELLA WHEELER WILCOX

# NIGHT AT SEA

*T*he lovely purple of the noon's bestowing
  Has vanished from the waters, where it flung
A royal color, such as gems are throwing
  Tyrian or regal garniture among.
'Tis night, and overhead the sky is gleaming,
  Thro' the slight vapor trembles each dim star;
I turn away—my heart is sadly dreaming
  Of scenes they do not light, of scenes afar.
    My friends, my absent friends!
      Do you think of me, as I think of you?

By each dark wave around the vessel sweeping
  Farther am I from old dear friends removed;
Till the lone vigil that I now am keeping,
  I did not know how much you were beloved.
How many acts of kindness little heeded,
  Kind looks, kind words, rise half reproachful now!
Hurried and anxious, my vexed life has speeded,
  And memory wears a soft accusing brow.
    My friends, my absent friends!
      Do you think of me, as I think of you?

The very stars are strangers, as I catch them
  Athwart the shadowy sails that swell above;
I cannot hope that other eyes will watch them
  At the same moment with a mutual love.
They shine not there, as here they now are shining;
  The very hours are changed. —Ah, do ye sleep?
O'er each home pillow midnight is declining—
  May some kind dream at least my image keep!
    My friends, my absent friends!
      Do you think of me, as I think of you?

Yesterday has a charm, Today could never
    Fling o'er the mind, which knows not till it parts
How it turns back with tenderest endeavor
    To fix the past within the heart of hearts.
Absence is full of memory, it teaches
    The value of all old familiar things;
The strengthener of affection, while it reaches
    O'er the dark parting, with an angel's wings.
      My friends, my absent friends!
        Do you think of me, as I think of you?

The world, with one vast element omitted—
    Man's own especial element, the earth;
Yet, o'er the waters is his rule transmitted
    By that great knowledge whence has power its birth.
How oft on some strange loveliness while gazing,
    Have I wished for you—beautiful as new,
The purple waves like some wild army raising
    Their snowy banners as the ship cuts through.
      My friends, my absent friends!
        Do you think of me, as I think of you?

Bearing upon its wings the hues of morning,
    Up springs the flying fish like life's false joy,
Which of the sunshine asks that frail adorning
    Whose very light is fated to destroy.
Ah, so doth genius on its rainbow pinion
    Spring from the depths of an unkindly world;
So spring sweet fancies from the heart's dominion—
    Too soon in death the scorched-up wing is furled.
      My friends, my absent friends!
        Whate'er I see is linked with thoughts of you.

No life is in the air, but in the waters
  Are creatures, huge, and terrible and strong;
The swordfish and the shark pursue their slaughters,
  War universal reigns these depths along.
Like some new island on the ocean springing,
  Floats on the surface some gigantic whale,
From its vast head a silver fountain flinging,
  Bright as the fountain in a fairy tale.
    My friends, my absent friends!
      I read such fairy legends while with you.

Light is amid the gloomy canvas spreading,
  The moon is whitening the dusky sails,
Fron the thick bank of clouds she masters, shedding
  The softest influence that o'er night prevails.
Pale is she like a young queen pale with splendor,
  Haunted with passionate thoughts too fond, too
    deep;
The very glory that she wears is tender,
  The very eyes that watch her beauty fain would weep.
    My friends, my absent friends!
      Do you think of me, as I think of you?

Sunshine is ever cheerful, when the morning
  Wakens the world with cloud-dispelling eyes;
The spirits mount to glad endeavor, scorning
  What toil upon a path so sunny lies.
Sunshine and hope are comrades, and their weather
  Calls into life an energy like Spring's;
But memory and moonlight go together,
  Reflected in the light that either brings.
    My friends, my absent friends!
      Do you think of me, then? I think of you.

The busy deck is hushed, no sounds are waking
    But the watch pacing silently and slow;
The waves against the sides incessant breaking,
    And rope and canvas swaying to and fro.
The topmast sail, it seems like some dim pinnacle
    Creating a shadowing tower amid the air;
While red and fitful gleams come from the binnacle,
    The only light on board to guide us—where?
        My friends, my absent friends!
            Far from my native land, and far from you.

On one side of the ship, the moonbeam's shimmer
    In luminous vibrations sweeps the sea,
But where the shadow falls, a strange, pale glimmer
    Seems, glow-worm like, amid the waves to be.
All that the spirit keeps of thought and feeling,
    Takes visionary hues from such an hour;
But while some fantasy is o'er me stealing,
    I start—remembrance has a keener power:
        My friends, my absent friends!
            From the fair dream I start to think of you.

A dusk line in the moonlight—I discover
    What all day long vainly I sought to catch;
Or is it but the varying clouds that hover
    Thick in the air, to mock the eyes that watch?
No; well the sailor knows each speck, appearing,
    Upon the tossing waves, the far-off strand;
To that dark line our eager ship is steering.
    Her voyage done—tomorrow we shall land.

LETITIA ELIZABETH MACLEAN

# FRIENDS FAR AWAY

*C*ount not the hours while their silent wings
   Thus waft them in fairy flight;
For feeling, warm from her dearest springs,
   Shall hallow the scene tonight.
And while the music of joy is here,
   And the colors of life are gay,
Let us think on those that have loved us dear,
   The Friends who are far away.

Few are the hearts that have proved the truth
   Of their early affection's vow;
And let those few, the beloved of youth,
   Be dear in their absence now.
O, vividly in their faithful breast
   Shall the gleam of remembrance play,
Like the lingering light of the crimson west,
   When the sunbeam hath passed away!

Soft be the sleep of their pleasant hours,
   And calm be the seas they roam!
May the way they travel be strewed with flowers
   Till it bring them in safety home!
And when we whose hearts are o'erflowing thus
   Ourselves may be doomed to stray,
May some kind orison rise for us,
   When we shall be far away!

HORACE TWISS

## TO A DISTANT FRIEND

$W$hy art thou silent! Is thy love a plant
Of such weak fiber that the treacherous air
Of absence withers what was once so fair?
Is there no debt to pay, no boon to grant?

Yet have my thoughts for thee been vigilant,
Bound to thy service with unceasing care—
The mind's least generous wish a mendicant
For nought but what thy happiness could spare.

Speak!—though this soft warm heart, once free to hold
A thousand tender pleasures, thine and mine,
Be left more desolate, more dreary cold
Than a forsaken bird's nest fill'd with snow
'Mid its own bush of leafless eglantine—
Speak, that my torturing doubts their end may know!

WILLIAM WORDSWORTH

# A LEGACY

*F*riend of my many years!
When the great silence falls, at last, on me,
Let me not leave, to pain and sadden thee,
   A memory of tears,

   But pleasant thoughts alone
Of one who was thy friendship's honored guest
And drank the wine of consolation pressed
   From sorrows of thy own.

   I leave with thee a sense
Of hands upheld and trials rendered less—
The unselfish joy which is to helpfulness
   Its own great recompense;

   The knowledge that from thine,
As from the garments of the Master, stole
Calmness and strength, the virtue which makes whole
   And heals without a sign;

   Yea more, the assurance strong
That love, which fails of perfect utterance here,
Lives on to fill the heavenly atmosphere
   With its immortal song.

JOHN GREENLEAF WHITTIER

## PARTED FRIENDS

*F*riend after friend departs:
   Who hath not lost a friend?
There is no union here of hearts
   That finds not here an end;
Were this frail world our only rest,
Living or dying, none were blest.

Beyond the flight of time,
   Beyond this vale of death,
There surely is some blessed clime
   Where life is not a breath,
Nor life's affections transient fire,
Whose sparks fly upward to expire.

There is a world above,
   Where parting is unknown;
A whole eternity of love,
   Formed for the good alone;
And faith beholds the dying here
Translated to that happier sphere.

Thus star by star declines,
   Till all are passed away,
As morning high and higher shines,
   To pure and perfect day;
Nor sink those stars in empty night;
They hide themselves in heaven's own light.

JAMES MONTGOMERY

## BENEDICITE

*G*od's love and peace be with thee, where
Soe'er this soft autumnal air
Lifts the dark tresses of thy hair!

Whether through city casements comes
Its kiss to thee, in crowded rooms,
Or, out among the woodland blooms,

It freshens o'er thy thoughtful face
Imparting, in its glad embrace,
Beauty to beauty, grace to grace!

Fair Nature's book together read,
The old wood paths that knew our tread,
The maple shadows overhead,—

The hills we climbed, the river seen
By gleams along its deep ravine,—
All keep thy memory fresh and green.

Where'er I look, where'er I stray,
Thy thought goes with me on my way,
And hence the prayer I breathe today:

O'er lapse of time and change of scene,
The weary waste which lies between
Thyself and me, my heart I lean.

Thou lack'st not Friendship's spellword, nor
The half-unconscious power to draw
All hearts to thine by Love's sweet law.

With these good gifts of God is cast
Thy lot, and many a charm thou hast
To hold the blessed angels fast.

If, then, a fervent wish for thee
The gracious heavens will heed from me,
What should, dear heart, its burden be?

The sighing of a shaken reed,—
What can I more than meekly plead
The greatness of our common need?

God's love,—unchanging, pure, and true,—
The Paraclete white-shining through
His peace,—the fall of Hermon's dew!

With such a prayer, on this sweet day,
As thou mayst hear and I may say,
I greet thee, dearest, far away!

JOHN GREENLEAF WHITTIER

## FAREWELL! BUT WHENEVER YOU WELCOME THE HOUR

*F*arewell! but whenever you welcome the hour
That awakens the night song of mirth in your bower,
Then think of the friend who once welcomed it too,
And forgot his own griefs to be happy with you.
His griefs may return—not a hope may remain
Of the few that have brightened his pathway of pain—
But he ne'er will forget the short vision that threw
Its enchantment around him while lingering with you!

And still on that evening, when pleasure fills up
To the highest top-sparkle each heart and each cup,
Where'er my path lies, be it gloomy or bright,
My soul, happy friends! shall be with you that night—
Shall join in your revels, your sports, and your wiles,
And return to me beaming all o'er with your smiles;
Too blest if it tells me that, mid the gay cheer,
Some kind voice had murmured, "I wish he were here!"

Let Fate do her worst, there are relics of joy,
Bright dreams of the past, which she cannot destroy!
Which come in the night-time of sorrow and care,
And bring back the features that joy used to wear.
Long, long be my heart with such memories filled!
Like the vase in which roses have once been distilled;
You may break, you may ruin the vase if you will,
But the scent of the roses will hang round it still.

THOMAS MOORE

# CAPE-COTTAGE AT SUNSET

*W*e stood upon the ragged rocks,
   When the long day was nearly done;
The waves had ceased their sullen shocks,
   And lapped our feet with murmuring tone,
And o'er the bay in streaming locks
   Blew the red tresses of the sun.

Along the West the golden bars
   Still to a deeper glory grew;
Above our heads the faint, few stars
   Looked out from the unfathomed blue;
And the fair city's clamorous jars
   Seemed melted in that evening hue.

O sunset sky! O purple tide!
   O friends to friends that closer pressed!
Those glories have in darkness died,
   And ye have left my longing breast.
I could not keep you by my side,
   Nor fix that radiance in the West.

Upon those rocks the waves shall beat
   With the same low and murmuring strain;
Across those waves, with glancing feet,
   The sunset rays shall seek the main;
But when together shall we meet
   Upon that far-off shore again?

W. B. GLAZIER

# WHEN TO THE SESSIONS OF SWEET
## SILENT THOUGHT

*W*hen to the sessions of sweet silent thought
I summon up remembrance of things past,
I sigh the lack of many a thing I sought,
And with old woes new wail my dear time's waste.
Then can I drown an eye, unused to flow,
For precious friends hid in death's dateless night,
And weep afresh love's long since cancelled woe,
And moan th' expense of many a vanished sight.
Then can I grieve at grievances foregone,
And heavily from woe to woe tell o'er
The sad account of fore-bemoanéd moan,
Which I new pay, as if not paid before;
But if the while I think on thee, dear friend,
All losses are restored, and sorrows end.

WILLIAM SHAKESPEARE

# THE FIRE OF DRIFTWOOD

*W*e sat within the farmhouse old,
   Whose windows, looking o'er the bay,
Gave to the sea breeze, damp and cold,
   An easy entrance, night and day.

Not far away we saw the port,—
   The strange, old-fashioned, silent town,—
The lighthouse,—the dismantled fort,—
   The wooden houses, quaint and brown.

We sat and talked until the night,
   Descending, filled the little room;
Our faces faded from the sight—
   Our voices only broke the gloom.

We spake of many a vanished scene,
   Of what we once had thought and said,
Of what had been, and might have been,
   And who was changed, and who was dead;

And all that fills the hearts of friends,
   When first they feel, with secret pain,
Their lives thenceforth have separate ends,
   And never can be one again;

The first slight swerving of the heart,
   That words are powerless to express,
And leave it still unsaid in part,
   Or say it in too great excess.

The very tones in which we spake
   Had something strange, I could but mark;
The leaves of memory seemed to make
   A mournful rustling in the dark.

Oft died the words upon our lips,
   As suddenly, from out the fire
Built of the wreck of stranded ships,
   The flames would leap and then expire.

And, as their splendor flashed and failed,
   We thought of wrecks upon the main,—
Of ships dismasted, that were hailed
   And sent no answer back again.

The windows, rattling in their frames,—
   The ocean, roaring up the beach,—
The gusty blast,—the bickering flames,—
   All mingled vaguely in our speech;

Until they made themselves a part
   Of fancies floating through the brain,—
The long-lost ventures of the heart,
   That send no answers back again.

O flames that glowed! O hearts that yearned!
   They were indeed too much akin—
The driftwood fire without that burned,
   The thoughts that burned and glowed within.

HENRY WADSWORTH LONGFELLOW

# WE HAVE BEEN FRIENDS TOGETHER

*W*e have been friends together,
  In sunshine and in shade;
Since first beneath the chestnut trees
  In infancy we played.
But coldness dwells within thy heart—
  A cloud is on thy brow;
We have been friends together—
  Shall a light word part us now?

We have been gay together;
  We have laughed at little jests;
For the fount of hope was gushing,
  Warm and joyous, in our breasts.
But laughter now hath fled thy lip,
  And sullen glooms thy brow;
We have been gay together—
  Shall a light word part us now?

We have been sad together—
  We have wept, with bitter tears,
O'er the grass-grown graves, where slumbered
  The hopes of early years.
The voices which are silent there
  Would bid thee clear thy brow;
We have been sad together—
  O! what shall part us now?

CAROLINE NORTON

## TO A FRIEND

*W*hen we were idlers with the loitering rills,
　The need of human love we little noted:
　Our love was nature; and the peace that floated
On the white mist, and dwelt upon the hills,
To sweet accord subdued our wayward wills:
　One soul was ours, one mind, one heart devoted,
　That, wisely doting, asked not why it doted,
And ours the unknown joy, which knowing kills.
But now I find how dear thou wert to me;
　That man is more than half of nature's treasure,
Of that fair beauty which no eye can see,
　Of that sweet music which no ear can measure;
　And now the streams may sing for others' pleasure,
The hills sleep on in their eternity.

HARTLEY COLERIDGE

# THE LIGHT OF OTHER DAYS

$O$ft in the stilly night
  Ere slumber's chain has bound me,
Fond Memory brings the light
  Of other days around me:
    The smiles, the tears
    Of boyhood's years,
  The words of love then spoken;
    The eyes that shone,
    Now dimm'd and gone,
  The cheerful hearts now broken!
Thus in the stilly night
  Ere slumber's chain has bound me,
Sad Memory brings the light
  Of other days around me.

When I remember all
  The friends so link'd together
I've seen around me fall
  Like leaves in wintry weather,
    I feel like one
    Who treads alone
  Some banquet hall deserted,
    Whose lights are fled
    Whose garlands dead,
  And all but he departed!
Thus in the stilly night
  Ere slumber's chain has bound me,
Sad Memory brings the light
  Of other days around me.

THOMAS HOOD

## THE PASSAGE

*M*any a year is in its grave,
Since I crossed the restless wave;
And the evening, fair as ever,
Shines on ruin, rock, and river.

Then in this same boat beside
Sat two comrades old and tried—
One with all a father's truth,
One with all the fire of youth.

One on earth in silence wrought,
And his grave in silence sought;
But the younger, brighter form
Passed in battle and in storm.

So, whene'er I turn my eye
Back upon the days gone by,
Saddening thoughts of friends come o'er me,
Friends that closed their course before me.

But what binds us, friend to friend,
But that soul with soul can blend?
Soul-like were those hours of yore;
Let us walk in soul once more.

Take, O boatman, thrice thy fee,—
Take, I give it willingly;
For, invisible to thee,
Spirits twain have crossed with me.

Ludwig Uhland

## THE OLD FAMILIAR FACES

*I* have had playmates, I have had companions
In my days of childhood, in my joyful school-days;
All, all are gone, the old familiar faces.

I have been laughing, I have been carousing,
Drinking late, sitting late, with my bosom cronies;
All, all are gone, the old familiar faces.

I loved a Love once, fairest among women:
Closed are her doors on me, I must not see her—
All, all are gone, the old familiar faces.

I have a friend, a kinder friend has no man:
Like an ingrate, I left my friend abruptly;
Left him, to muse on the old familiar faces,

Ghost-like I paced round the haunts of my childhood,
Earth seem'd a desert I was bound to traverse,
Seeking to find the old familiar faces.

Friend of my bosom, thou more than a brother,
Why wert not thou born in my father's dwelling?
So might we talk of the old familiar faces,

How some they have died, and some they have left me,
And some are taken from me; all are departed;
All, all are gone, the old familiar faces.

CHARLES LAMB

# THE DEAD FRIEND

*From "In Memoriam"*

*T*he path by which we twain did go,
   Which led by tracts that pleased us well,
   Through four sweet years arose and fell,
From flower to flower, from snow to snow.

· · · · ·

But where the path we walked began
   To slant the fifth autumnal slope,
   As we descended following Hope,
There sat the Shadow feared of man;

Who broke our fair companionship,
   And spread his mantle dark and cold,
   And wrapped thee formless in the fold,
And dulled the murmur on thy lip.

· · · · ·

I know that this was Life,—the track
   Whereon with equal feet we fared;
   And then, as now, the day prepared
The daily burden for the back.

But this it was that made me move
   As light as carrier-birds in air;
   I loved the weight I had to bear
Because it needed help of Love:

Nor could I weary, heart or limb,
   When mighty Love would cleave in twain
   The lading of a single pain,
And part it, giving half to him.

· · · · ·

But I remained, whose hopes were dim,
   Whose life, whose thoughts were little worth
   To wander on a darkened earth,
Where all things round me breathed of him.

O friendship, equal-poised control,
　O heart, with kindliest motion warm,
　O sacred essence, other form,
O solemn ghost, O crownéd soul!

Yet none could better know than I,
　How much of act at human hands
　The sense of human will demands
By which we dare to live or die.

Whatever way my days decline,
　I felt and feel, though left alone,
　His being working in mine own,
The footsteps of his life in mine.

　·　·　·　·　·

My pulses therefore beat again
　For other friends that once I met;
　Nor can it suit me to forget
The mighty hopes that make us men.

I woo your love: I count it crime
　To mourn for any overmuch;
　I, the divided half of such
A friendship as had mastered Time;

Which masters Time, indeed, and is
　Eternal, separate from fears:
　The all-assuming months and years
Can take no part away from this.

　·　·　·　·　·

The hills are shadows, and they flow
　From form to form, and nothing stands;
　They melt like mist, the solid lands,
Like clouds they shape themselves and go.

But in my spirit will I dwell,
　And dream my dream, and hold it true;
　For though my lips may breathe adieu,
I cannot think the thing farewell.

ALFRED TENNYSON

## ON THE DEATH OF
## JOSEPH RODMAN DRAKE

*G*reen be the turf above thee,
   Friend of my better days!
None knew thee but to love thee,
   Nor named thee but to praise.

Tears fell when thou wert dying,
   From eyes unused to weep,
And long, where thou art lying,
   Will tears the cold turf steep.

When hearts, whose truth was proven,
   Like thine, are laid in earth,
There should a wreath be woven
   To tell the world their worth;

And I who woke each morrow
   To clasp thy hand in mine,
Who shared thy joy and sorrow,
   Whose weal and woe were thine;

It should be mine to braid it
   Around thy faded brow,
But I've in vain essayed it,
   And feel I cannot now.

While memory bids me weep thee,
   Nor thoughts nor words are free,—
The grief is fixed too deeply
   That mourns a man like thee.

FITZ-GREENE HALLECK

# AULD LANG SYNE

*S*hould auld acquaintance be forgot,
    And never brought to min'?
Should auld acquaintance be forgot,
    And days o' lang syne?

> For auld lang syne, my dear,
>     For auld lang syne,
>   We'll tak a cup o' kindness yet
>     For auld lang syne.

We twa hae rin about the braes,
    And pu'd the gowans fine;
But we've wandered monie a weary fit
    Sin' auld lang syne.

We twa hae paidl't i' the burn,
    Frae mornin' sun till dine;
But seas between us braid hae roared
    Sin' auld lang syne.

And here's a hand, my trusty fiere,
    And gie's a hand o' thine;
And we'll tak a right guid willie-waught
    For auld lang syne.

And surely ye'll be your pint-stowp,
    And surely I'll be mine,
And we'll take a cup o' kindness yet
    For auld lang syne!

ROBERT BURNS

## SALAAM ALAIKUM

*(Peace Be With You)*

*I* pray the prayer the Easterners do,
May the peace of Allah abide with you.
Wherever you stay, wherever you go,
May the beautiful palms of Allah grow.
Through days of labor and nights of rest,
The love of good Allah make thee blest.
So I touch my heart as the Easterners do,
May the peace of Allah abide with you.

Author Unknown